TO KNOW THE KNOWER

SWAMI MUKTANANDA

Published by SYDA Foundation
PO Box 600, South Fallsburg, New York 12779, USA

Design by Derek Beecham
Cover illustration by Christian Kaviiik Gavignet

Second edition, 1993

Copyright © 1979, 1993 SYDA Foundation®. All rights reserved.

No part of this book may be reproduced or transmitted in any form or by
any means, electronic or mechanical, including photocopy, recording, or any information
storage and retrieval system, without prior written permission from SYDA Foundation,
Permission Department, PO Box 600, South Fallsburg, New York 12779, USA.

(Swami) MUKTANANDA, (Swami) CHIDVILASANANDA, GURUMAYI, SIDDHA MEDITATION,
and SIDDHA YOGA are registered service marks of SYDA Foundation in the USA.

Printed in the United States of America.

ISBN: 0-914602-91-8

TO KNOW THE KNOWER

SWAMI MUKTANANDA

A SIDDHA YOGA MEDITATION PUBLICATION
PUBLISHED BY SYDA FOUNDATION

Swami Muktananda

SWAMI MUKTANANDA
AND THE SIDDHA LINEAGE

Swami Muktananda was born in 1908. When he was still a schoolboy, he met Bhagawan Nityananda, the ecstatic saint whom he would later recognize as his Master. Soon afterward, the boy was overcome by an intense desire for a direct experience of the Truth. And so, at the age of fifteen, he left home to begin a life of seeking. He went first to the ashram of a great Siddha Master named Siddharudha Swami. There he took initiation into *sannyāsa*, or monkhood, receiving the name Swami Muktananda, which means the "bliss of liberation." For the next thirty years he traveled the length and breadth of India, searching for the Master who could give him the experience of God.

But the Truth he sought eluded him—until he came to the feet of the great Siddha Master whom he had met so many years before. Bhagawan Nityananda was an austere, utterly detached, overwhelmingly powerful being in whose presence all became silent. Recognizing him as the Guru he had sought, Swami Muktananda devoted himself to a life of discipleship. From Bhagawan Nityananda he received Shaktipat, the sacred

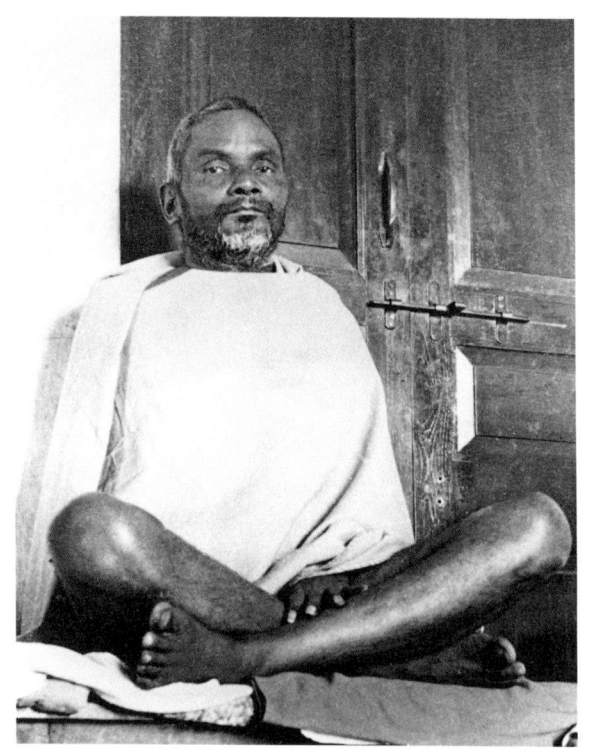

Bhagawan Nityananda

initiation of the Siddha tradition, which awakened his inner Kundalini energy.

This began a nine-year period of intense internal transformation during which Swami Muktananda passed through all the stages of meditation. In 1956, he reached the culmination of his years of practice, attaining the state of Self-realization. Still, he continued to live as a simple disciple in Ganeshpuri, the small village where his Guru had settled. Then, in 1961, Bhagawan Nityananda took *mahāsamādhi*—the scriptural term for the passing of a saint. Before leaving the world, he transmitted the power of the Siddha lineage to Swami Muktananda, investing him with the full potency of his own tremendous spiritual attainment.

Baba, as he came to be known, made his first trip abroad in 1970. This was the beginning of a remarkable worldwide mission. Empowered by his Guru to give Shaktipat initiation, Baba Muktananda awakened unprecedented numbers of people, of all ages and backgrounds, to the experience of their own inner divinity.

For many years Baba prepared his successor, Gurumayi Chidvilasananda. She first met him as a child of five. The

Gurumayi Chidvilasananda

loving bond of Guru and disciple was instantaneously formed. Later, when he made his tours of the West, Gurumayi traveled with him, serving him in innumerable ways.

In 1982, these years of rigorous preparation culminated when Baba bequeathed to her the full power and knowledge of the Siddha lineage, the vast spiritual legacy which his own Guru had passed on to him. A few months later, Baba Muktananda took mahasamadhi, merging into the ultimate state of union with the Absolute.

When Gurumayi was still a young girl, Baba said of her, "She is a great flame. One day she will illumine the world." Now, as the Master of the Siddha lineage, Gurumayi bestows the treasured gift of Shaktipat, awakening the inner Kundalini energy of seekers of all nationalities. With this awakening comes a new understanding of our lives, which uplifts and transforms them and leads, in the end, to enlightenment—the goal of human life.

There is nothing more pure
or more sublime than knowledge,
because it is knowledge
which reveals the inner Self to you.

Knowledge is the light of the inner Self.
From knowledge comes supreme happiness.

For a person of knowledge,
it is very easy to attain the Self.

For a person of ignorance,
it is very difficult.

The Self doesn't belong to any action,
technique, or path.
The Self belongs to right understanding.

It is the understanding of Truth
which revels as Consciousness in everything.

Through knowledge of the Self
comes understanding of Consciousness
and the Self is attained.

With great cleverness you may say,
"I know this person,
I know that person,
I know everybody."
However,
as long as you don't know your own Self
you don't know anybody;
you only know your own delusion.

You may think you understand everything
but no matter in what field you may work,
if you don't understand your own Self
then you only understand
your own self-deception.
Eventually,
you claim your non-understanding
to be understanding.

We should have the understanding
of true understanding.
When we know our own Self,
then we know right knowledge
and we know everything.

The source of all knowledge
is the state of the Self.

It is the life of all life.
It is eternal peace and happiness.
It is love.
It arises from its own bliss.

Someone once asked me,
"What constitutes the Self?"
I told him,
"If something constitutes the Self
then what good is the Self?"
The Self is spontaneous,
Self-made and eternal.
The Self makes everything else, too.
It is the Consciousness that supports
and knows everything.

It is just like a painting on a wall.
First comes the wall;
then comes the picture.

On Consciousness your picture is drawn.

There is a being inside you
who knows everything.
Try to understand Him.
He is Consciousness.
He is the Self. He is God.
Because He exists, you exist.

He is the experience of "I am."

In the beginning
there is only I-consciousness.
All other things are added later.

As the pure "I," He is the supreme Truth.
Mansur called Him *anal-Haqq*.
Shankaracharya called Him
aham Brahmāsmi.
Muktananda Swami calls Him "I am That."

He is the Knower.
He is inside you.
He makes the breath move.
He makes your eyes open and close.
He inspires the tongue to speak.

But even though He lives in this body
He knows He is different from the body.

He is called the experiencing subject,
the seer.

At night you are fast asleep
but He is awake.
He reports to you next morning
what you dreamt,
how you slept.

So perceive the One who is always awake,
the inner witness.
He is the Self.

Do you want to know God as He is?
Or do you only want to know God
as your mind tells you He is?

How can a flashlight illuminate the sun?
How can you know the Knower of the mind
with the mind?

He is nothing but knowledge and light.
He illuminates everything inside.

He will never come under the control
of your mind
because He is the mind of the mind,
the intellect of the intellect,
the subconscious of the subconscious,
and the ego of the ego.

So many thoughts arise and subside,
arise and subside.
Try to perceive the source
of the arising and subsiding thoughts.
When the waves of thoughts stop arising,
that is the space of God.
God lies at the source of thoughts.
He is the Knower and knows everything.

If you make a lot of effort,
if you do a lot of sadhana
you may not find Him.

You will know Him
the moment you understand Him.

Without knowledge,
without recognition,
you have nothing.

It is said that even a rich man
without knowledge of his wealth
is a pauper.

The Self gives its knowledge to you
all the time.
You just don't recognize it.

All you have to do is see
that which you already have.
Enlightenment is yours.
It is only a matter of understanding.

I don't tell you to attain the Self.
You have already attained it.
I tell you to attain
the knowledge of the Knower.

To know the Knower is meditation
and the highest truth.
It is enlightenment.

Ultimately, you will realize
the Knower is Brahman,
the known is Brahman,
the process of knowing is Brahman,
and you are Brahman.

Just as with its own light
the sun illuminates the world and itself,
so you are the source of all knowledge.

Only the Self can know the Self.
Only God can know God.
You are that Self.
You are that God.

If you keep pondering this knowledge,
it will soon start vibrating within you.
It will pervade and permeate
your entire system.
Then, whenever you need its help,
it will come alive in you.

Remember,
without form, color, shape, sign, or symbol,
God is the embodiment of knowledge.

Still, all forms, colors,
shapes, signs, and symbols
belong to Him and are Him.

Though He is not anything,
He is everything.

He is in your heart.
You lost Him in your heart;
you will find Him only in your heart.

In everyone's heart
there lies a wish-fulfilling tree,
the supreme Self.

Siddha Yoga makes you experience
this Self within you
immediately.

I bless you
so that the wisdom and knowledge
of Siddha Yoga
may bear fruit for you.

Perhaps you are afraid of losing yourself;
but without losing yourself
nothing can be attained.
I can assure you that when you lose yourself,
you will find something.

Go ahead, lose yourself.
I will find you.

Love of God is the greatest worship.
Love of one's fellow man
is the greatest love of God
and the highest knowledge.

It is Consciousness itself
which has created this world
from its own inspiration
and which dwells inside you.

Honor and love your own being
and then let that love spread to others.
Meditate on your own Self,
know your own Self
and all knowledge will be yours.

I love you and welcome you
with all my heart,
knowing your inner Consciousness is God.

SYDA Publications

Ashes at My Guru's Feet
Kindle My Heart, Volumes I & II
From the Finite to the Infinite, Volumes I & II
I Am That
I Have Become Alive
Play of Consciousness
Kundalini: The Secret of Life
Secret of the Siddhas
Siddha Meditation
Does Death Really Exist?
Where Are You Going?
Light on the Path
The Perfect Relationship
Mukteshwari
Satsang with Baba
Reflections of the Self
In the Company of a Siddha
Mystery of the Mind
Meditate
Getting Rid of What You Haven't Got
I Love You
The Self Is Already Attained
A Book for the Mind
I Welcome You All With Love
God Is With You

For more information about translation editions and books by Swami Muktananda and Gurumayi Chidvilasananda, write to Siddha Yoga Meditation Bookstore, PO Box 600, South Fallsburg, NY 12779, USA.

SIDDHA YOGA MEDITATION ASHRAMS AND CENTERS

Siddha Yoga Meditation is practiced in more than 600 ashrams and centers throughout the world. For more information, contact:

GURUDEV SIDDHA PEETH
PO Ganeshpuri PIN 401-206
District Thana, Maharashtra
India

SIDDHA YOGA
GLOBAL COMMUNICATIONS
DEPARTMENT
PO Box 600
South Fallsburg, NY 12779
USA
Tel. (914) 434-2000